How To Not Always Be Working

WORK LESS EARN MORE!

Learn The Tricks To Working Smart Right Now For More Time Freedom

ERIC FREEMAN

Table of Contents

Chapter 1: Why Are You Working So Hard.. 6
Chapter 2: Who Are You Working For? 10
Chapter 3: Fight Is The Reward.. 13
Chapter 4: Everything is A Marathon Not A Sprint............................... 16
Chapter 5: The Only Obstacle Is Yourself... 20
Chapter 6: You Will Never Regret Good Work Once It is Done......... 24
Chapter 7: Things That Spark Joy 27
Chapter 8: Structure Your Day With Tasks You Excel At and Enjoy 30
Chapter 9: Having a Balanced Life.. 32
Chapter 10: 10 Habits Of The Rich And Successful............................. 35
Chapter 11: How To Take Action.. 40
Chapter 12: 6 Habits of The Mega-Rich... 45
Chapter 13: The Lure of Wanting Luxury Items................................... 49
Chapter 14: Only Buying Things that serve a purpose For you 53
Chapter 15: How To live Your Best Life 55
Chapter 16: The Problem With Immediate Gratification...................... 58
Chapter 17: Happy People Don't Sweat the Small Stuff. 63
Chapter 18: 5 Tips to Doing Unique and Meaningful Work 66
Chapter 19: Stop Lying To Yourself.. 70
Chapter 20: 8 Ways To Gain Self-Confidence 73
Chapter 21: **Start Working On Your Dreams Today**....................... 77
Chapter 22: *7 Ways On How To Attract Success In Life* 81
Chapter 23: 10 Habits of Drake.. 85
Chapter 24: Happy People Don't Make Excuses................................... 90
Chapter 25: 10 Habits of Successful Traders 92
Chapter 26: The Appetite of Success 97
Chapter 27: Planning Ahead... 99

Chapter 28: How to Learn Faster 102
Chapter 29: 6 Habits To Impress Your Boss and Thrive 105
Chapter 30: The Struggle With Time 109
Chapter 31: The Power of Growing 1% Each Day 112
Chapter 32: How To Take Note of Your Flaws 115
Chapter 33: 10 Habits of David Beckham 117
Chapter 34: How To Live In The Moment 122

Chapter 1:
Why Are You Working So Hard

Your why,
your reason to get up in the morning,
the reason you act,
really is everything - for without it, there could be nothing.
Your why is the partner of your what,
that is what you want to achieve, your ultimate goal.
Your why will be what pushes you through the hard times on the path to your dreams.

It may be your children or a burning desire to help those less fortunate,
whatever the reason may be,
it is important to keep that in mind when faced with troubles or distractions.

Knowing what you want to do, and why you are doing it,
is of imperative importance for your life.
The tragedy is that most people are aiming for nothing.
They couldn't tell you why they are working in a certain field even if they tried.
Apart from the obvious financial payment,
They have no clue why they are there.

Is financial survival alone really a good motive to act?
Or would financial prosperity be guaranteed if you pursued greater personal preference?
Whatever your ambitions or preference in life,
make sure your why is important enough to you to guarantee your persistence.

Sometimes when pursuing a burning desire,
we can become distracted from the reason we are working.

Your why should be reflected in everything you do.
Once you convince yourself that your reason is important enough, you will not stop.
Despite the hardships, despite the fear, despite the loss and pain.
As long as you maintain a steady path of faith and resilience,
your work will soon start to pay off.
A light will protrude from the darkness and the illusionary troubles sent to test your faith will disappear as if they were never here.

Your why must be strong.
Your what must be as clear as the day is to you now.
And your faith must be eternal and unwavering.
Only then will the doors be opened to you.
This dream can be real, and will be.

When it is clear in the mind with faith, the world will move to show you the way.

The way will be revealed piece by piece, requiring you to take action and do the required work to bring your dream into reality.

Your why is so incredibly important.
The bigger your why, the greater the urgency, and the quicker your action will be.

Take the leap of faith.
Do what you didn't even know you could.
Never mind anyone else.
Taking the unknown path.
Perhaps against the advice of your family and friend,
But you know what your heart wants.

You know that even though the path will be dangerous, the reward will be tremendous.
The risks of not never finding out is too great.
The risk of never knowing if you could have done better is unfathomable.
You can always do better, and you must.

Knowing what is best for you may prove to be the most important thing for you.
How you feel about the work you are doing,
How you feel about the life you are living,
And how do you make the most of the time you have on this earth.
These may prove far more important than financial reward could ever do for you.

Aim to strike a balance.

A balance between working on what you are passionate about and building a wealthy financial life.

If your why and will are strong enough,

Success is all but guaranteed for you – no second guesses needed.

Aim for the sky,

However high you make it,

you will have proven you can indeed fly.

Chapter 2:
Who Are You Working For?

Who you work for is up to you,

but ultimately every person has a choice in that decision.

Whether you are self-employed, self-made, or salaried,

You determine your own destiny.

As Earl Nightingale said, only the successful will admit it.

You might work for one company your whole life,

but ultimately you are still working for yourself and your family.

If you do not like the practices of your company,

you have the power to leave and make a change.

You must choose to serve who you believe to be worthy of your life.

High self-esteem stops successful people ever feeling subordinate to anyone.

Achieve your goals by envisioning yourself providing quality service in the companies and places that will maximise your chances of success.

Always view yourself as equal to everybody.

All of us have unique talents and qualities within us.

Acknowledg that we can learn from anybody.

Nobody is above or below us.

You can build such qualities that are keys to success.

If one client is taking all your time, reassess his or her value.
If the contract is no longer rewarding, end it as soon as possible.
Doesn't matter if it is a business or personal relationship.

You must get clear on the fact that you are working for you.
You should consider no one your boss.
You should view whoever pays you as a client,
As such you should provide them the best service you can.

Always look to create more opportunity for your business.
Don't look for security - it doesn't exist.
Even if you find it for a time, I guarantee it will be boring at best.

Look for productivity and progression.
Change is definite. It is the only constant.
It will be up to you whether it is progression or regression.

Work with people who have similar goals and objectives.
You should always work with, never for.
Remember that you are always working for yourself.

If working with a company is not bringing you any closer to your goal,
End it now and find one that will.
You should never feel stuck in a job because leaving it is only a letter or phone call away.
You can replace that income in a million different ways.

If you don't like someone scheduling your week for you, start your own business.
If you don't know how, get the training.
Investing in your skills is an investment in your future.

Learning doesn't end with high school.
That was only the beginning – that was practice
Be a life-long learner.
Learn on the job.
Learn so you can achieve more.

Once you admit that you are working for you,
change your bosses title to 'client'.
Open your eyes to a world of other big and wonderful opportunities.

Realize that you are more valuable than you previously believed yourself to be.
Believe you will are incredibly valuable, and you deserve to be paid accordingly.

Whether you are a minimum wage worker or a company director,
you probably haven't even scratched the surface of your capabilities.

Every time someone places limits on what is possible, somebody proves them wrong.
You work for yourself, the possibilities are limitless.

Chapter 3:
Fight Is The Reward

There are times in our lives when we feel blocked out. When we feel the darkness coming in. When we see the sun going down and seemingly never coming back up. When the winds feel tougher and everything coming in your way puts you down like a storm.

No matter how big and how defiant you get, life will always find a new way to knock you down.

You will often find yourself in a place where you have nowhere to go, but straight. And that straight path isn't always the easiest too. It has all these ridges and peaks or a long ditch. So you finally come to realize that the only way out is a challenge itself and you can't bow out because there is no other way around.

I want you to understand the concept of fight and struggle. The success stories and breakthroughs we all hear are mostly just 2 parts; its 90% work and 10% fight.

We all work and we all work hard. But the defining moment of our journey is the final fight we go through.

The work we put in gets us to the bottom of the final barrier but the effort we need to summit the peak is the fight we put in and finally get the breakthrough. But fighting isn't easy. It is the hardest part of your journey to success.

The fight you need to put in isn't just the Xs and O's. The true fight is your mental toughness. It's your sheer will to keep going and keep pushing because you are just around the corner for the ultimate success.

You are just on the verge of finding the best reward of your life. You are on the cusp of seeing and enjoying your happiest moments. Because you have finally found your dreams and you have finally fulfilled your purpose in life.

Now is the time to rise and give up the feeling of giving up. Now is the time to get on top of your challenges. Now is the time to sweat and get over that pain.

This is the moment you need to be at your best. This is the time you need your A-game. This is the time to defy all odds and go all in. Because the finals moments need the final straw of strength and effort in your body.

Make a decision and become your own light. Believe in yourself like you have never before and you will never look back.

So if you ask me again why is fighting worth it. It's because your attitude makes you win long before you have even set the foot in the battleground. It's your will to keep going that makes you stand out even before getting into the spotlight.

You don't win a fight when you fight, you win a fight before the fight even begins. Your ultimate reward is the collection of all your efforts and resilience.

Chapter 4:
Everything is A Marathon Not A Sprint

Ask your parents, what was it like to raise children till the time they were able to lift their weight and be self-sufficient. I am sure they will say, it was the most beautiful experience in their lives. But believe me, They are lying.

There is no doubt in it that what you are today is because of your parents, and your parents didn't rest on their backs while a nanny was taking care of you.

They spent countless nights of sleeplessness changing diapers and soothing you so that you can have a good night's sleep. They did that because they wanted to see a part of them grow one day and become what they couldn't be. What you are today is because of their continuous struggle over the years.

You didn't grow up overnight, and your parents didn't teach you everything overnight. It took years for them to teach you and it took even more time for you to learn.

This is life!

Life is an amalgamation of little moments and each moment is more important than the last one.

Start with a small change. Learn new skills. The world around you changes every day. Don't get stuck in your routine life. Expand your horizons. What's making you money today might not even exist tomorrow. So why stick to it for the rest of your life.

You are never too old to learn new things. The day you stop learning is the last day of your life. A human being is the most supreme being in this universe for a reason. That reason is the intellect and the ability to keep moving with their lives.

You can never be a millionaire in one night. It's a one-in-billion chance to win a lottery and do that overnight. Most people see the results of their efforts in their next generation, but the efforts do pay off.

If you want to have eternal success. It will take an eternity of effort and struggles to get there. Because life is a marathon and a marathon tests your last breaths. But when it pays off, it is the highest you can get.

Shaping up a rock doesn't take one single hit, but hundreds of precision cuts with keen observation and attention. Life is that same rock, only bigger and much more difficult.

Changing your life won't happen overnight. Changing the way you see things won't happen overnight. It will take time.

To know everything and to pretend to know everything is the wrong approach to life. It's about progress. It's about learning a little bit at each step along the way.

To evolve, to adapt, to figure out things as they come, is the process of life that every living being in this universe has gone through before and will continue to go through in the future. We are who we are because of the marathon of life.

Every one of us today has more powerful things in our possessions right now than our previous 4 generations combined. So we are lucky to be in this world, in this era.

We have unlimited resources at our disposal, but we still can't get things in the blink of an eye. Because no matter how evolved we are, we still are a slave to the reality of nature, and that reality is the time itself!

If you are taking each step to expect a treat at each stop, you might not get anything. But if you believe that each step that you take is a piece in a puzzle, a puzzle that becomes a picture that is far beautiful and meaningful, believe me, the sky is your limit.

Life is a set of goals. You push and grind to get these goals but when you get there you realize that there is so much more to go on and achieve.

Committing to a goal is difficult but watching your dreams come true is something worth fighting for.

You might not see it today, you might not see it 2 years from now, but the finish line is always one step closer. Life has always been and always will be a race to the top. But only the ones who make it to the top have gone through a series of marathons and felt the grind throughout everything.

Your best is yet to come but is on the other end of that finish line.

Chapter 5:
The Only Obstacle Is Yourself

Ever wondered why you feel low all the time?
Why it seems like everyone is better than you?
Why everyone excels at something that you wished you were good at too?

I am sure you have wondered about at least one of these at one or another instance in your life.

These questions remain unanswered no matter how hard you try. Until you realize that the only answer that fits the puzzle is that, it is because of you.

All these barriers and limitations are placed upon you not because you are stupid or incapable.
It is merely because you have limiting beliefs about yourself that stop you from achieving your fullest potential.
It is because you are not trying hard enough to make yourself stand apart from everyone else in the world.

If you lag at school, study hard.
If your lag at your job, socialize more.
If you are obese, break a sweat to lose all that fat.

If you lack some technical skill, learn till you beat the very best in that field.

Don't blame others for your failures.
Everyone else starts off with the same resources and expertise as you.
If others can succeed, Why can't you?
Who is stopping you from flying high in victory?
If no one else tells you, let me do the honors; it's you.

You are the biggest cause of everything that is happening in your life right now.
Nothing is good or bad unless you do or don't do something to generate that result.

Make a promise to yourself today that you will achieve something great by the end of this week.
Envision the big picture and start watching yourself get drawn into that picture.

Take baby steps. take a big leap of faith.
Move one foot forward over the other no matter how big or small.
Once you get past the fear of being stuck where you currently are,
life will start opening great doors to your every step forward.

Sometimes we may take a step back.
Sometimes life throws us durians instead of lemons.

As long as you dust yourself off and move again you are never going to lose.

Don't idealize someone if you are not ready to idealize yourself.
To envision yourself charting your own path, in your own unique pair of shoes.

If for whatever reason you don't achieve that something someday, don't beat yourself up for it.
Maybe those shoes weren't the right fit for you.
Try another pair of shoes, and walk down a new path with confidence.

This could be a blessing in disguise for you.
A lesson for you to strive towards something new.
Something better. Something that no one has ever dreamed of or done before.

If along the way some someone comes and tells you to stop, and you stop to hear them say that to you, it wasn't their fault, but yours. Because you were idle enough to be distracted by others to compromise that dream.

Don't lift your head until you have achieved something today. Don't say a word to anyone about your goals.

Spend more and more time to figure out your life. Promise yourself that no one else matters in your life till you have achieved everything and you are left with nothing more to achieve.

I remember the time my father told me to be a better man than him. The time when I fell off my bicycle for the first time. He came to me and said, 'Don't give up now, as you will fall every day, but when you rise you will achieve bigger and better things than you could ever wish'.

My father gave me his hand when I needed it the most and he still does. But when he is gone and there is no one free enough or caring enough left to see me go through all that struggle, then I will be the closest figure to my father to back me up and give me the courage to get up and start again till I succeed in riding the bike of life.

You and I are capable of riding the high tide. Either we ride it all the way to the shore or we drown to never get back up again. It's up to us now what we want to do. It's you who decides what you were and what you can be!

You will regret yourself the most when you finally come to realize that it was 'You' who brought you down. So don't waste yourself and make a vow today, a vow to be the best you can be and the rest will be history.

Chapter 6:
You Will Never Regret Good Work Once It is Done

Humans have debated the same things for thousands of years. More than often we get split within ourselves for whether this is right or if we are wrong. The question should never be about right or wrong. It should always be about if it suits us and others for the greater good.

Most of us spend our lives finding the answers to the questions that are born within our instincts and natural trait of curiosity. We work hard for these answers but rarely are we get satisfied with what we are doing.

We have made it so hard for ourselves to come to terms with our basic nature and level of work.

We always try to go one step ahead of others and try to prove ourselves the others. When we really should be getting more indulged in our self and our passions to get a better grip of what is going around in our lives and our loved ones.

We don't have to be proven right if we want to be content because this one approval is just the beginning.

Doing good things for the sake of just being superior is an ugly deed. But doing it for the greater good of everyone is a deed to be proud of. You should feel proud if you make someone happy but you should regret if at any time you start feeling superior for doing good.

Staying humble is the best trait a human can scrub. Even if you have all the wealth in the world.

But the thing to remember above all is that whatever you do, and whatever the outcome is, you should never feel bad or regret anything. If your intentions are pure and you put your best out there, you have no reason to feel crushed or devastated.

Life tests us in every way possible. It slaps us just when we are the most vulnerable. But the diamonds are the most difficult gems to mine. You will always find the best outcome in the harshest situations.

You only have to make sure that you don't judge your deeds based on morality, Rather you rate your efforts on a humanitarian level.

Your nature is expansive, unlike the animals with basic instincts and desires. You have to expand and explore your emotional abilities and you must try to find the deeper corners of your personality that you still haven't discovered.

Life can reward you even in the smallest of efforts. Happiness can be found in even the smallest shortest smiles that you cause.

Happiness has no definite cause, except for good intentions and the will to keep doing those things without a single grain of self profit.

But regret and shame can take root from the smallest of cracks in your will. So make sure to fill those cracks and you will turn into a skyscraper one day. Hang in there and these days will pass too.

Chapter 7:
Things That Spark Joy

I'm sure you've heard the term "spark joy", and this is our topic of discussion today that I am going to borrow heavily from Marie Kondo.

Now why do I find the term spark joy so fascinating and why have i used it extensively in all areas of my life ever since coming across that term a few years ago?

When I first watched Marie Kondo's show on Netflix and also reading articles on how this simple concept that she has created has helped people declutter their homes by choosing the items that bring joy to them and discarding or giving away the ones that don't, I began my own process of decluttering my house of junk from clothes to props to ornaments, and even to furniture.

I realised that many things that looked good or are the most aesthetically pleasing, aren't always the most comfortable to use or wear. And when they are not my go to choice, they tend to sit on shelves collecting dust and taking up precious space in my house. And after going through my things one by one, this recurring theme kept propping up time and again. And i subconsciously associated comfort and ease of use with things that spark joy to me. If I could pick something up easily without hesitation to use or wear, they tend to me things that I gravitated to naturally, and these things began to spark joy when i used them. And when i started getting rid of things that I don't find particularly pleased to use, i felt my house was only filled with enjoyable things that I not only enjoyed looking at, but also using on a regular and frequent basis.

This association of comfort and ease of use became my life philosophy. It didn't apply to simply just decluttering my home, but also applied to the process of acquiring in the form of shopping. Every time i would pick something up and consider if it was worthy of a purpose, i would examine whether this thing would be something that I felt was comfortable and that i could see myself utilising, and if that answer was no, i would put them down and never consider them again because i knew deep down that it would not spark joy in me as I have associated joy with comfort.

This simple philosophy has helped saved me thousands of dollars in frivolous spending that was a trademark of my old self. I would buy things on the fly without much consideration and most often they would end up as white elephants in my closet or cupboard.

To me, things that spark joy can apply to work, friends, and relationships as well. Expanding on the act of decluttering put forth by Marie Kondo. If the things you do, and the people you hang out with don't spark you much joy, then why bother? You would be better off spending time doing things with people that you actually find fun and not waste everybody's time in the process. I believe you would also come out of it being a much happier person rather than forcing yourself to be around people and situations that bring you grief.

Now that is not to say that you shouldn't challenge yourself and put yourself out there. But rather it is to give you a chance to assess the things you do around you and to train yourself to do things that really spark joy in you that it becomes second nature. It is like being fine tuned to your 6th sense in a way because ultimately we all know what we truly like and dislike, however we choose to ignore these feelings and that costs us time effort and money.

So today's challenge is for you to take a look at your life, your home, your friendships, career, and your relationships. Ask yourself, does this thing spark joy? If it doesn't, maybe you should consider a decluttering of sorts from all these different areas in your life and to streamline it to a more minimalist one that you can be proud of owning each and every piece.

Chapter 8:
Structure Your Day With Tasks You Excel At and Enjoy

For those who have been doing their own thing for a while, we know that it is not easy to put together a day that is truly enjoyable. We forget about doing the things we like and excel at, and start getting lost in a sea of work that we have to drag ourselves through doing.

If we don't have a choice, then I guess we can't really do anything about it. But if we do, we need to start identifying the tasks that require the most attention but the least effort on our part to do. Tasks that seem just about second-nature to us. Tasks that we would do even if nobody wanted to pay us. Tasks that allow our creativity to grow and expand, tasks that challenge us but not drain us, tasks that enriches us, or tasks that we simply enjoy doing.

The founding father of modern Singapore, one of the wealthiest countries in the world, Mr Lee Kuan Yew once said, find what works and just keep doing it over and over again. I would apply that to this situation as well. We have to find what works for us and just double down on it. The other stuff that we aren't good at, either hire someone else to do it, or find a way to do less of it or learn how to be good at it fast. Make it a challenge for ourselves. Who knows maybe you might find them enjoyable once you get a hang of it as well.

But for those things that already come naturally to us, do more of it. Pack a lot of time into at the start of the day. Dedicate a few hours of your day to those meaningful tasks that you excel at. You will find that once you get the creative juices and the momentum going, you will be able to conquer the other less pleasing tasks more easily knowing that you've already accomplished your goals for the day.

Start right now. Identify what those tasks that you absolutely love to do right now, work-wise, or whatever it may be, and just double down on it. Watch your day transform.

Chapter 9:
Having a Balanced Life

Today we're going to talk about how and why you should strive to achieve a balanced life. A balance between work, play, family, friends, and just time alone to yourself.

We all tend to lead busy lives. At some points we shift our entire focus onto something at the expense of other areas that are equally important.

I remember the time when I just got a new office space. I was so excited to work that i spent almost 95% of the week at the office. I couldn't for the life of me figured why i was so addicted to going to the office that I failed to see I was neglecting my family, my friends, my relationships. Soon after the novelty effect wore off, i found myself burnt out, distant from my friends and family, and sadly also found myself in a strained relationship.

This distance was created by me and me alone. I had forgotten what my priorities were. I hadn't realized that I had thrown my life completely off balance. I found myself missing the time I spent with my family and friends. And I found myself having to repair a strained relationship due to my lack of care and concern for the other party.

What you think is right in the moment, to focus on something exclusively at the expense of all else, may seem enticing. It may seem like there is nothing wrong with it. But dig deeper and check to make sure it is truly worth the sacrifice you are willing to make in other areas of your life.

It is easy for us to fall into the trap of wanting to make more money, wanting to work harder, to be career driven and all that. But what is the point in having more money if you don't have anyone to spend in on or spend it with? What's the point in having a nice car or a nice designer handbag if you don't have anyone to show it to?

Creating balance in our lives is a choice. We have the choice to carve out time in our schedule for the things that truly matter. Only when we know how to prioritise our day, our week, our month, can we truly find consistency and stability in our lives.

I know some people might say disagree with what I am sharing with you all today, but this is coming from my personal life experience. It was only after realising that I had broken down all the things I had worked so hard to build prior to this new work venture, that I started to see the bigger picture again.

That I didn't want to go down this path and find myself 30 years later regretting that I had not spent time with my family before they passed away, that I was all alone in this world without someone I can lean my shoulder on to walk this journey with me, that I didn't have any friends that I could call up on a Tuesday afternoon to have lunch with me because everyone thought of me as a flaker who didn't prioritise them in the their lives before.

Choose the kind of life you want for yourself. If what I have to say resonates with you, start writing down the things that you know you have not been paying much attention to lately because of something else that you chose to do. Whether it be your lover, your friends, a hobby, a passion project, whatever it may be. Start doing it again. The time to create balance is now.

Chapter 10:
10 Habits Of The Rich And Successful

The rich and successful have common habits. Some of them have walked down the same path to glory.

Wealth is not measured in terms of properties only but also the strength of character. One can be rich in wisdom but not as much in properties. Nevertheless, they are considered rich and successful because they have an abundance of an intangible asset – wisdom.

Here are ten habits of the rich and successful:

1. <u>They Are Generous</u>

Rich and successful people are often generous because they know what it feels like to lack. Even those born in rich families are generous because they probably have seen their parents helping the needy.

Most rich people globally have foundations in their name. It is not a channel to wealth for themselves, but a means to do acts of charity. The Bill & Melinda gates foundation, for example, has helped the most vulnerable globally during a famine, war, and even during the coronavirus disease pandemic.

2. <u>They Read Widely</u>

Successful people read a lot. The reading culture in them developed at an early age and could have most likely molded them into the people they are. Great leaders are readers. As leaders of giant corporates, it is important to be well vast with the wisdom of other great people.

Reading is not capped at any age. Successful people know that learning is continuous and apply the knowledge from the literature they read in their lives. Reading lightens the burden of management on the shoulders of the rich who are directors in their companies.

3. They Are Not Workaholics

It is amazing how one can be wealthy and successful without being a workaholic. Ironically, most workaholics are not as rich as you would expect. Despite them foregoing a lot of things for the sake of their work, they cannot match the rich who work only a few hours a day.

It is not the amount of time you work but the quality of work you do. Work holism will rob you of your social life and you will be depressed. Apportion equal time in everything you do, not only your work.

4. They Are Social People

One would think that most rich and successful people are arrogant or anti-social. This is untrue. They are social and outgoing. You will find them in their social circles over coffee or playing golf. They are approachable and receptive to new ideas.

Reaching them is indeed difficult because of their security or protocol to follow before talking to them. They have security because of their high profile and they could be targets of bad people. Nevertheless, they are very engaging when you get to know them.

5. They Have Trust Issues

Most rich people are insecure because of their wealth. They rarely trust strangers because their intentions are unknown. Some of them have been shortchanged in their business dealings and cannot easily trust again.

When interacting with them, do not take offense to their mistrust. Instead, try to win their trust slowly until they realize that you are genuine. It is only then that they will trust you with their work or build a friendship with you.

6. They Are Never Idle

An idle mind is the devil's workshop. The rich and successful know this too well. You may be tempted into doing immoral acts when you have a lot of idle time at your disposal. Engage yourself willfully in productive activities lest you are lured into vices because you have a lot of free time. This is not a call to work holism. It is okay to have free time to spend out of your busy schedule, but that time should be planned for carefully. Like the rich and successful, your mind should always be occupied with positive thoughts and plans on how you can progress.

7. They Have A Flexible Mindset

The rich and successful do not lead rigid lives. They have a flexible mindset that makes them open to other business ideas and suggestions. Their ears listen to consumer needs in the market and they develop products and services to meet those needs.

It is often misconceived that successful people live in their zone and are indifferent to common people. The truth is that they became successful by being open-minded. A fixed mind is an enemy of progress.

8. They Are Bold

Wealthy people are bold and make public statements without any fear of backlash. Boldness is a sign of being an alpha.

As much as their wealth could be insulation against any repercussions, people pay attention when the rich give their opinions because they are unsure of their motive. When a successful person boldly gives their opinion, it is taken seriously because it has the potential to influence market forces.

9. They Consult Widely

The rich are not always wise; even the wise seek counsel. Before they make any significant action, they seek advice from people they trust. They then weigh the pros and cons of what they intended to do and make an informed choice.

Unlike common people who act out of impulse, the rich take advice from trusted sources (mostly professionals) very seriously. Rarely do they err, always hitting the nail on the head. You should consider consulting before acting if you want to be like the rich.

10. They Are Visionary

Vision is often misconstrued for sight. It is getting the bigger picture without losing grip on fine details. Were it not for the eagle vision of the successful, they could not be able to maintain their status. Rich people know the direction they are going and they work towards it.

Vision is not an innate trait; it is developed over time. You will need to be visionary and not get distracted as you chart your way towards richness. Take this cue from successful people.

In conclusion, we acknowledge that the rich and successful run the world. When you start practicing their habits, you will soon be like them.

Chapter 11:
How To Take Action

Today we're going to talk about something pretty crucial. And this also plays into the topics of motivation, purpose, and goals. And that is, "How To Take Action". Before we begin, i want you to write down a couple of things that you were supposed to take action on but have been putting it off for whatever reason. And i want you to keep these things in mind as we go through this video. And hopefully by the end of it, i would have been able to convince you to take action and to start moving forward in your bigger life projects as well.

Why is Taking Action so important? To put it simply, taking action is the one thing that we can control to move us towards our goals. Whether we succeed or not is irrelevant in this case. Many of us hesitate to take action because we are afraid of failure. We fear the unknown and we over analyse and over think things to a point that we become paralysed. And I'm sure you guys have heard this term before: and that is analysis paralysis.

We draw up such detailed plans for how to are going to tackle this problem, we tweak and tweak the draft, aiming to find perfection before we even take the first action step to begin doing the work. And many times, for many people, we just let the plan sit on the shelves or in our computer, afraid to take action because we fear that we might not be able to accomplish the goal we have set out for ourselves.

You see, planning and drafting isn't going to move the needle. When we have a project, planning only makes up a small part of the process. And completion of the project is always down to every member of the group taking action and completing their part of the task. Or in the case of a solo project, all of the action and effort put in comes from you.

When we plan for anything, even for our future, it is something that keeps us in check, to have a reference for us to know that we are on the right track. But whether or not we follow those plans are entirely up to the actions that we actually take. Whether we do save that $100 every month, or not spend money on unnecessary things, or say that we are going to invest in constant education and growth, these are not set in stone if we do not take action.

Another thing that holds us back from taking action is the fear that we will make mistakes. And that we will feel like a fool if we did things wrongly. But if you look at your life, realistically, how many times have you actually done something right the first time around on something that you haven't actually tried before? For example riding a bike, swimming, learning a new language, learning a new instrument. Wouldn't you agree that making mistakes is actually part of the process? Without practice there's not perfect, so why do we think that we will always get it right the first time when it comes to starting a new business or taking action on whatever new thing that we had set our sights on?

We have no problem telling ourselves that making mistakes in smaller things is okay but we berate ourselves or we create this immense expectation that we must get things right the first time around on bigger projects that we fear the climb because we fear the thought of falling down. And we don't even give ourselves a chance to prove that we can do it.

To counter this, we must tell ourselves that making mistakes is a part of the process, to not rush the process, and to give ourselves more room for failure so that we will have the best chance of actually succeeding someday. However long it takes. We must trust the process because it will happen for us eventually. The only time we really do fail is the last time we actually stop trying, stop taking action, and stop learning from our mistakes. that is the time when we can say we are a failure, if we quit. But if we never give up, and we keep taking action, it will work out for us.

One final hurdle that many of us face is that we tend to want to rush the process and we set unrealistic deadlines to achieve those goals. If we go back to our previous example of learning a new instrument, how many of you guys will agree that, although not impossible, it is unrealistic to become a guitar guru after the 1st year? Most of us would realistically say that it will take at least a few years of daily practice to actually become a pro guitar player. But how many of us actually apply that same concept to a big project like growing our income from $3k to $10k. We all expect fast results and fast growth, but rarely does things work out so smoothly, unless we are incredibly lucky.

When we set these big targets but fail to realise that we need to take baby steps consistently everyday, we set ourselves up for failure without realising it. Without giving ourselves the room to grow a seed into a tree, we end up chopping it down when it is still at the early growth stages. And we fail to let time and effort do it's thing, giving it water and light day in and day out. And we beat ourselves up when we quit prematurely.

What I have learnt, from experience, is that the best way to achieve something eventually, is to take baby steps, taking a little action each day, be it 5 mins, an hour, or 10 hours, they all count. And instead of just hoping to rush to the end, that I actually learned to not only enjoy the process, but also to trust that my efforts will all pay off in the end. And many a times, they did. I left the fear and worry to one side and just focused on taking action. I stopped comparing myself with my peers, and focused on my own journey. I can't control how much faster my competition can grow or achieve, but i can definitely control my own destiny.

So i challenge each and everyone of you today to take a look at the list of things that you hope to achieve that you have written down at the start of this video, and to take the first step of stop trying to perfect the plan, to stop thinking and worrying about what might and could go wrong, to stop fearing the unknown, and to simply just take a little action each day. The worse thing that you can do to yourself is to not even try. You will make mistakes along the way, but as long as you learn from them, you will be moving in the right direction.

Chapter 12:

6 Habits of The Mega-Rich

There are rich people then there are the mega-rich. The distinction between them is as clear as day. The former are still accumulating their wealth while the latter is beyond that. Their focus is no longer on themselves but humanity. Their view of things is through the prism of business and not employment. Their business enterprises are well established and their level of competition is unmatched. They are at the top of the pyramid and have a clear view of things below.

Here are six habits of the mega-rich:

1. <u>They Have a Diversified Investment Portfolio</u>

The mega-rich are ardent followers of the saying "do not put all your eggs in one basket." They have stakes in every type of business across many world economies beginning with their country. Their patriotism makes them not leave out their countries when they do business.

With diversified risk across various sectors of the economy, they can remain afloat even during tough economic times. Their companies and businesses also yield high returns because of proper management and their diversification.

2. <u>They Are Generous</u>

The mega-rich people are generous to a fault. They run foundations and non-governmental organizations in their name with a cause to help humanity. It indicates their generosity and desire to help the most vulnerable and needy in society. Generosity is a hard trait to trace these days and it distinguishes the mega-rich from kind people.

The generosity of mega-rich people seeks to help the needy permanently by showing them how to fish instead of giving them fish. Such an act liberates families from poverty and promises a brighter future to the younger generation.

3. They Are Neither Petty Nor Trivial

Pettiness is not the character of mega-rich people. They do not have time for small squabbles and fights. Instead, they use their energy in pursuit of more productive goals. Their minds always think of their next big move and ways to improve their businesses. They do not have time to engage in non-issues.

Mega-rich investors do not undertake trivial investments. Their businesses are major leaving people marveling at its grandiose. Jeff Benzos took a trip to space and the world was amazed. The impact the ilk of Benzos has in the world economy is unmatched; securities exchanges and global trade shakes whenever such people make a business move.

4. They Have A Clean Public Image

The mega-rich people manage to maintain a scandalous-free public image. This is crucial for their success. When was the last time you came across a character-damaging story of a wealthy person? It is difficult to recall. Perception tends to stick in the minds of people more than reality. This makes it important for them to guard their reputation with their life. If you are on the path of joining the exclusive club of the mega-rich, begin cleaning up your reputation if it is a mess. Build a new public image that will portray you as a better person to the world. Mega-rich people intimidate by their angel-like reputations and immense influence on their social status.

5. <u>They Have Great Character</u>

A man's character precedes his reputation. Every wealthy person upgrades his/hers. The mega-rich treasure character too much because they are unable to buy it at any price. It is invaluable. Characterlessness is a type of poverty only curable the hard way. There is no shortcut to it except tireless and intentional channeling of your efforts to strengthen it. A great character is an asset envied by the great and mighty because most of them fall short of it. There are untold stories of the efforts mega-rich people put to build their character. This has formed part of their routine and life habit.

6. <u>They Champion Global Causes</u>

Mega-rich people are champions of social justice and world causes like climate change and global warming. They give their contribution towards global causes without any self-interest. They are at the forefront offering support in whatever capacity.

They invest in these worthy causes because of the duty of corporate social responsibility they owe the world. It is not a debt they pay but an act they do gladly because they have the best interest of the world at heart.

These six habits of the mega-rich have formed their lifestyle. Walk in their footsteps if you want to become like them. You will command respect from everybody. Your business moves shall determine world market trends and you shall set the pace in every sector of the economy.

Chapter 13:
The Lure of Wanting Luxury Items

Have you ever walked by a store and pondered over those LV bags if you were a lady? Secretly hoping that you can get your hands on one of those bags so that you can feel good about yourself when you carry them on your shoulders? Or have you ever glanced at a boutique watch shop if you were a guy hoping that you can get your hands on one of the rolexes which costs north of $10k minimum? That could be the same lust and desire for the latest and greatest cars, apple products, clothing, etc. anything you name it.

You think of saving up a year's worth of salary just to be able to afford one of these things and you see yourself feeling good about it and that you can brag to your friends and show off to people that you have the latest and most expensive product on the market. and you imagine yourself being happy that it is all you will need to stay happy.

I am here to tell you that the lure of owning luxury items can only make you happy to a certain extent. And only if purchasing these things is something of great meaning to you, like achieving a big milestone that you want to commemorate in life. In that instance, walking into that store to purchase that luxury product can be a great experience and of great significance as well. Whether it be a birthday gift to yourself, or commemorating a wedding anniversary, job/career work milestone, or any of that in nature, you will tend to hold these products with great sentimental value and hardly will you ever sell these items should the opportunity arise to make a profit from them (which is generally not the case with most things you buy).

I will argue that when you pick these products to wear from your wardrobe, you will indeed be filled with feelings of happiness, but it is not the product itself that makes you happy, but it is the story behind it, the hard work, the commemorative occasion that you will associate and remember these products for. It will transport you back in time to that place in your life when you made the purchase and you will indeed relive that emotion that took you there to the store in the first place. That to me is a meaningful luxury purchase that is not based on lust or greed, but of great significance.

But what if you are just someone who is chasing these luxury products just because everyone else has it? When you walk down the street and you see all these people carrying these products and you just tell yourself you have to have it or else? You find all the money you can dig from your savings and emergency fund to pay for that product? I would argue that in that instance, you will not be as happy as you thought you would be. These kinds of wants just simply do not carry the weight of any importance. And after feeling good for a few days after you owned that luxury good, you feel a deep sense of emptiness because it really does not make you a happier person. Instead you are someone trying to have something but with that comes a big hole in your wallet or your bank account. The enthusiasm and excitement starts to fade away and you wonder whats the next luxury good you need to buy to feel that joy again.

You see, material goods cannot fill us with love and happiness. Luxury goods are only there to serve one purpose, to reward you for your hard work and that you can comfortably purchase it without regret and worry that you are left financially in trouble. The lure of many of us is that we tend to want what we can't have. It could also turn into an obsession for many of us where we just keep buying more and more of these luxury goods to satisfy our craving for materialistic things. You will realise one day that the pursuit never ends, the more you see, the more you want. And that is just how our brains are wired.

I have a confession to make, I had an obsession for apple products myself and I always thought I wanted the latest and greatest apple products every year when a new model comes out. And every year apple seems to know how to satisfy my lust for these products and manages to make me spend thousands of dollars every time they launch something new. This addiction i would say lasted for a good 8 years until I recently realised that the excitement ALWAYS fades after a week or two. Sure it is exciting to play with it for a couple of days while your brain gets used to this incredible piece of technology sitting in front of you. But after a week or two, I am left wondering, whats next? I began to realise that what really made me happy was doing what i love, engaging in my favourite hobbies, meeting friends, and just living simply without so many wants in life. When you have less wants, you automatically go into a mindset of abundance. And that is a great feeling to have.

I challenge all of you today to question what is your real motivation behind wanted to buy luxury items. Is it to commemorate a significant achievement in your life? or is it a meaningless lust for something that you want to emulate others for. Dig deeper and you will find the answer. Thank you

Chapter 14:
Only Buying Things that serve a purpose For you

Today I'm going to talk about the right way to buy things. The right way to shop. The right way to spend your hard earned money.

You see, many of us think that we need to buy things to make working hard at our jobs worth the effort. Sure it does help, in the form of retail therapy for some, but a lot of times we end up just excessively buying things that clutter up our house, our space, our homes. Stuff that we only use once and never touch again. Clothes is a common way that this kind of hoarding happens. We don't notice it because we are buying one shirt or one pants at a time, but over just a few shopping sprees and we find our closets full to the brim. And we never wear some of these clothing's more than once, but we throw the "old" ones to make way for the new.

I believe that the right way to buy things is only to purchase quality items that truly deserve a spot in our homes. Things that bring us joy. Things that we are 1000% sure we will use regularly.

For me, I love apple products. I admit that this one area is where I spend most of my money. I may not buy clothes, shoes, bags, but i will definitely put down money to buy apple products. The thing though is that I only buy items that serve a purpose for me in everyday things that I do. As a music lover, i loved their audio products and the ease of which I can enjoy my favourite music and tv shows with their devices. And I use these products on a daily basis. Everytime i pick up an apple product, i find it such a joy to use.

If you get that same feeling with a particular item, it is okay to get it. I'm not here to tell you u shouldnt be buying anything. As long as it is within your means and you know it will not end up untouched for months, then by all means get it. If something doesn't serve you anymore, sell it, donate it away, keep your space free of clutter.

A clutter-free home can provide enormous benefits for our mental and emotional health. To quote Marie Kondo, and to go one step further, only buy things that truly spark joy in you. Never buy things just because. You may feel good in the moment to splurge, but that feeling won't last. Pick your battles and pick your items carefully.

Chapter 15:
How To live Your Best Life

This is a simple yet not easy topic to tackle. But I am sure that this question is something that all of you are aspiring to achieve in life. Because really, being on earth, being alive, it does not have any real significance if we do not live it to our fullest potential, to enjoy every single wonderful thing that life has to offer, to smell the flowers, to see the sights along the way, and to appreciate the little things while going for the big dreams.

For many of us, I do believe that it was a lot easier to live our best life while we were in school. Whilst the pressure of school and getting good grades were always constantly hanging over us, that was the case for every other kid around us. It was fair game. And we all strived to be the best student that we could possibly be. At the same time we had time to pursue our interests, learn new things, learn new skills, and even new instruments. The possibilities were endless and the world was our oyster. We explored the deepest oceans and in my opinion, we were indeed living our best lives as children and teens.

Making friends and hanging out with them frequently either through study or play weren't difficult. We were social creatures and we were really good at that.

However as we grew older, into our twenties and beyond, we start to lose that spark. That wonder. That curiosity. That vision that the world was in the palm of our hands. Instead, that view became more myopic, it keeps shrinking, work gets in the way, and we lose our sense of wonder and curiosity. We become more cynical and dull. And we stopped really trying to live our best life.

The introvert in us starts to come out more and more, and we retreat into our homes watching Netflix and YouTube, rather than going out there into the world and doing something significant or fun. In today's topic we are not going to talk about careers or income, because i do not believe that you need to be incredibly successful monetarily to be described as living your best life. But rather it's the other things that make up who you are that matters here.

And for many of us, it has become all too easy to retreat into the comfort of our home after a long day's work and decide that it is perfectly good to just lay on our couches and do nothing all day or weekend. We gradually disconnect ourselves from the outside world and we live in our own little bubble. And we think it is okay.

However what we fail to realize is that over time, these hours add up to days, weeks, months, and even years. And we realise that at the end of it all, we have nothing to show for it. We have not put ourselves in positions where we are exposed to new experiences and things. Of fostering meaningful friendships that would last u to till the end of your life. And we find ourselves alone and regretting that we had not utilised our time more wisely to build up those relationships or creating those experiences that we can look back on and say I'm glad i did all those things. I'm glad i left no stone unturned. I'm glad i did not waste my time doing nothing.

So to sum it all up, i believe that to live your best life, we should all look back at our middle school and high school days. What were we doing then that made everything so interesting and exciting, and how can we integrate more of that into our lives instead of choosing isolation. Whether that be trying out a new activity, learning a new sport, or even simply just hanging out with friends that you can rely on on a much more regular basis. I do believe that you will start to feel that life has much more meaning and happiness will soon follow.

Chapter 16:
The Problem With Immediate Gratification

In today's topic we are going to talk about something that I am sure most of us struggle with every single day, myself included. I hope that by the end of this video, you will be able to make better decisions for yourself to maybe think further ahead rather than trying to get gratification right away.

There will be 5 areas that I want to talk about. Finance, social media, shopping, fitness, and career.

Alright if you're ready let's begin.

Let's start with the one thing that i think most of us will find it hard to resist. Shopping. For many of us, buying things can be a form of happiness. When we want something, our dopamine levels rise, and our attention is solely focused on acquiring that object whatever it may be. The anticipation of getting something is something very exciting and our bodies crave that sense of gratification in getting that product. Shopping can also be a form of distraction, maybe from work or from feeling stressed out. Shopping can also arise from boredom and the desire within us to satisfy our cravings for wanting things begins to consume us. This creates a real problem because after we attain the item, often we are not satisfied and start looking for the next thing. This creates a never ending cycle of seeking gratification immediately at the expense of our bank account. And we are soon left with a big hole in the wallet without realising it.

Before I talk about the solutions to this problem, i want to address the other 4 areas on the list.

The next one is social media. We tend to gravitate towards social media apps when we want to fill our time out of most probably boredom. At times when we are supposed to be working, instead of blocking out time to stay focused on the task at hand, we end up clicking on Instagram or Facebook, trying to see if there are any new updates to look at provided to us by the algorithm. Social media companies know this and they exploit our feeble nature with this cheap trick. Everytime we try to refresh a page, we seek immediate gratification. And we create within us a terrible habit hundreds of times a day, checking for updates that wastes hours away from our day.

The next area that maybe isn't so common is in the area of fitness. Instead of laying out a long term plan to improve our health and fitness through regular exercise and choosing healthy foods, we tend to want things happening for us immediately. We think and crave losing 10 pounds by tomorrow and set unrealistic targets that easily lets us down. Hence we seek for quick fix solutions that aim to cut short this process. We may end up trying to take slimming pills, or looking for the next extreme fad or diet to get to our goals quicker. Many of them not ending the right way and can be potentially harmful for our health. For those that cannot control what they eat, in reverse they may seek immediate gratification by bingeing on a fast food meal, ice cream, chocolates, or whatever foods brings them the quickest source of comfort. Many a times at the expense of their weight. All these are also very harmful examples of immediate gratification.

The 4th area I want to talk about is something of bigger importance. And this may not resonate with everybody, but it is about having a career that also focuses on building a side stream of passive income rather than one that focuses on active income. You see active income is static. When we work, we get a pay check at the end of every month. We look forward to that paycheck and that becomes our gratification. But when we stop working, our income stream ceases as well. This desire to keep that paycheck every month keeps us in the jobs that we ate. And we only look towards our jobs as a means to an end, to get that gratification every month in X amounts of dollars. And for many of us who uses shopping as a way to fill the void left by our jobs, we end up using that Hard earned money to gratify ourselves even more, taking up loans and mortgages to buy more and more things. If this is you, you are definitely not alone.

The final area I want to address in the area of finance. And that goes hand in hand with spending money as well. You see for many of us, we fail to see the power that compounding and time has on our finances. When we spend money today instead of saving or investing it, we lose the potential returns that investments can do for our capital. While it may be fun for us to spend money now to acquire things, it may instead bring us 10x the joy knowing that this $1000 that we have invested could end up becoming $100000 in 30 years when it is time for us to retire. The effects of compounding are astonishing and I urge all of you to take a closer look at investing what you have now as you might be surprised at the amounts of returns you can get in 30-50 years or even sooner.

So where does this lead us in our fight against instant gratification? From the areas we have described, immediate gratification always seem to have a direct negative consequence. When we choose to satisfy our cravings for wanting things fast right now, we feed our inner desires that just keeps craving more. The point is that we will never be satisfied.

If however we take a long-term approach to things and make better decisions to delay our reward, many a times that feeling will return us more than 2 fold than if we had taken it immediately. The problem is that most of us do not possess this sort of patience. Our instinct tells us that now is the best time. But history and the law of life has repeatedly shown us that that is not always true. For many things in our life, things actually gets better with time. The more time you give yourself to heal from a heartbreak, the better it will get. The more time you invest your money, the greater the returns. The more time you spend time on doing something you love, the more happiness you will feel. The more time you put into eating moderately and exercising regularly, the faster you will see your body and health take shape. The more you resist turning on the social media app, the more you will find you won't need its attention after a while. The more time you spend with friends, the deeper the friendship.

The moral of the story in all of this is that giving yourself enough time is the key to success. Trying to get something quick and easy is not always the best solution to everything. You have to put in the time and energy required to see the fruits of your labour. And that is a law that we all have to realise and apply if we want to see true success. Rome isn't built in a day, so why would anything else be? We shouldn't rush through everything that we do expecting fast results and instant gratification.

So i challenge each and everyone of you to take a good look at the areas of your life that you expect fast results and things to happen immediately. See if any of the things that I have mentioned earlier resonates with you and see if you can modify the way you acquire things. I believe that with a little effort, we all can look towards a more rewarding path to success.

Thank you, I hope you learned something today and I'll see you in the next one.

Chapter 17:
Happy People Don't Sweat the Small Stuff.

Stress follows a peculiar principle: when life hits us with big crises—the death of a loved one or a job loss—we somehow find the inner strength to endure these upheavals in due course. It's the little things that drive us insane day after day—traffic congestion, awful service at a restaurant, an overbearing coworker taking credit for your work, meddling in-laws, for example.

It's all too easy to get caught up in the many irritations of life. We overdramatize and overreact to life's myriad tribulations. Under the direct influence of anguish, our minds are bewildered, and we feel disoriented. This creates stress, which makes the problems more difficult to deal with.

The central thesis of psychotherapist Richard Carlson's bestselling *Doesn't Sweat The Small Stuff… And It's All Small Stuff* (1997) is this: to deal with angst or anger, we need not some upbeat self-help prescriptions for changing ourselves, but simply a measure of perspective.

Perspective helps us understand that there's an art to understand what we should let go of and what we should concern ourselves with. It is important to focus our efforts on the important stuff and not waste time on insignificant and incidental things.

I've previously written about my favorite [5-5-5 technique](#) for gaining perspective and guarding myself against [anger erupting](#): I remove myself from the offending environment and contemplate if whatever I'm getting worked up over is of importance. I ask myself, "Will this matter in 5 days? Will this matter in 5 months? Will this matter in 5 years?"

Carlson stresses that there's always a vantage point from which even the biggest stressor can be effectively dealt with. The challenge is to keep making that shift in perspective. When we achieve that ["wise-person-in-me" perspective](#), our problems seem more controllable and our lives more peaceful.

Carlson's prescriptions aren't uncommon—we can learn to be more patient, compassionate, generous, grateful, and kind, all of which will improve the way we feel about ourselves and how other people feel when they are around us.

Some of Carlson's 100 recommendations are trite and banal—for example, "make peace with imperfection," "think of your problems as potential teachers," "remember that when you die, your 'in-basket' won't be empty," and "do one thing at a time." Others are more informative:

- Let others have the glory
- Let others be "right" most of the time
- Become aware of your moods, and don't allow yourself to be fooled by the low ones
- Look beyond behavior
- Every day, tell at least one person something you like, admire, or appreciate about them.
- Argue for your limitations, and they're yours
- Resist the urge to criticize
- Read articles and books with entirely different points of view from your own and try to learn something.

Chapter 18:
5 Tips to Doing Unique and Meaningful Work

When you think about meaningful work, you think about Mother Theresa or Princess Diana or maybe Peace Corp workers or school teachers and nurses. All of these are great and meaningful jobs. But, not everyone can raise money and attention to help get landmines cleared, nor can (or should) everyone try to teach second grade. And if blood makes you faint, nursing isn't a great idea for you either.

So, how can you make your job meaningful work, even when it's not directly making anyone's life better? These five suggestions will change your job from tedious work to meaningful work.

1. Look at the Big Picture

Why does your job exist? You could be an HR manager, a grocery store cashier, or a tech company CEO. Each of these jobs is necessary to make the world a better place.

Because this is no longer an agrarian society, you need the grocery store cashier to get food. CEOs of well-managed companies provide goods and services to the community and jobs with paychecks for many people. And HR managers can make people's lives much better by helping them progress in their careers, finding and providing the best benefits, and hiring great people.

If you just look at the tasks in front of you, you'll forget how you contribute to the community as a whole.

2. Treat Each Other With Kindness

A kind person can change everyone's day from drudgery to fun. Yes, work is still working, and sometimes it's hard, but working with the right people can make you look forward to working even if the job is hard work.

One man who worked for a brewery as a delivery man could have seen his job as hard work and struggle. After all, his job duty was to drive from restaurant to restaurant, carrying huge kegs of beer and taking out the old, empty ones. But, the people in many restaurants cheered when the beer guy came in with the beer kegs. Their act of kindness changed his job from drudgery to one that he loved.

3. Work Hard

How does working hard make a job meaningful? Well, hard work often equals success. When you succeed in your job, you help others in your department succeed in their jobs. When your whole department succeeds, the company succeeds. That is pretty meaningful.

Additionally, hard work is easier than avoiding work. Think about it: when you have to worry if your boss knows how much time you're spending surfing the internet, that adds another layer of complexity to your job. When you're working hard all of the time, and your boss drops by, it's not a big deal.

When you keep on top of your work, you have lowered stress levels. Now, of course, some people are overburdened and cannot accomplish everything. You might start feeling like, "I can't get everything done, so why bother?" These feelings of stress and failure can pose a huge temptation, but don't give in. First of all, you'll start to feel like your job just isn't meaningful—it's just work. Second, that adds additional stress on top of your head.

What you do instead is go to your boss and say directly, "I have five tasks on my plate right now. I can do four effectively, or I can do a lousy job on all five. Which would you prefer?" or "I have five tasks on my plate right now. I only have time to get three of them done. Which two should I skip?"

4. Look Outside of Your Job

Does your meaningful work have to be your day job? Of course not. Sometimes your day job can fund your meaningful work. Work-life balance means having a life. Whether it's through your family, church, charity, art, or whatever is important to you, you need a paycheck to support that.

You don't have to fulfill all of your needs through your paid job. You don't even need to feel guilty that you're working for a large corporation rather than a small non-profit. It's not bad to earn money. You find your meaning in how you can spend that money.

5. Consider Changing Jobs

If you just can't see how your current job is meaningful, and you can't figure out a way to make your job meaningful work, then perhaps it's time for you to move on. If your job doesn't bring you joy, doesn't allow you to support your family or essential charitable causes, and doesn't help the community, then maybe it's not the right job for you.

No one has a skill set that is so tiny and unique that there is only one job in the world that would suit them. And if you have no marketable skills, get training in new skills. You don't have to invest in a college degree if that's not your goal.

Chapter 19:
Stop Lying To Yourself

What do you think you are doing with your life? What do you keep on telling everyone you are up to? What ambitions do you make for yourself? What ideas do you follow? What goals do you want to follow and do you really have no choice in any of these?

These are not some random rude questions one might ask you. Because you deserve all of them if you still don't have anything meaningful in your life to stand behind.

You need to find a real achievement in your life that can make you feel accomplished.

Life is always a hard race to finish line with all of us running for the same goal of glory and success. But not all of us have the thing that will get us to that line first. SO when we fail to get there, we make reasons for our failure.

The reality is that it is never OK to make excuses for your failure when you weren't even eligible to join others to start with.

You have been lying to yourself this whole time, telling yourself that you have everything that takes to beat everyone to that finish line!

You have been lying to yourself saying that you are better than anyone there who came well prepared!

You keep telling yourself that you have a better understanding of things that you have just seen in your life for the first time! That you have a better approach towards life. That you know the best way to solve any problem.

Well, guess what my friend, You are wrong!

You don't have it all in you, you never did and you would probably never will. Because no man can master even one craft, let alone every. You need to do your homework for everything in your life, you try to master everything you come across but you can never really do so because you are a human. It is humanly impossible to be perfect at everything.

So stop calling yourself a saint or a self-taught genius because you are not.

You have this habit of lying to yourself because you find an escape from your faults. You find a way to cope with your inabilities. You find a way to soothe yourself that you are not wrong, just because everyone else says so.

You have to understand the fact that life has a way to be lived, and it is never the way of denial. It is rather the hopeful and quiet way of living your life with hard work and freedom.

You have to make your life worth living for. Because you know it in the back of your head that you have done the necessary hard work before to be able to compete among the best of the best out there.

You must have a strong feeling of justice towards yourself and towards others that makes you feel deserving of the highest honors and the biggest riches. Because you worked your whole life to be able to stand here and be a nominee for what life has to offer the best

Chapter 20:
8 Ways To Gain Self-Confidence

Confidence is not something that can be inherited or learned but is rather a state of mind. Confidence is an attribute that most people would kill to possess. It comes from the feelings of well-being, acceptance of your body and mind (your self-esteem), and belief in your ability, skills, and experience. Positive thinking, knowledge, training, and talking to other people are valuable ways to help improve or boost your confidence levels. Although the definition of self-confidence is different for everyone, the simplest one can be 'to have faith and believe in yourself.'

Here are 8 Ways To Gain More Self-Confidence:

1. **Look at what you have already achieved:**

It's easy to lose confidence when we dwell on our past mistakes and believe that we haven't actually achieved anything yet. It's common to degrade ourselves and not see our achievements as something special. But we should be proud of ourselves even if we do just a single task throughout the day that benefited us or the society in any way. Please make a list of all the things you are proud of, and it can be as small as cleaning your room or as big as getting a good grade or excelling in your job. Keep adding your small or significant achievements every day. Whenever you feel low in confidence, pull out the list and remind yourself how far you have come, how many amazing things you have done, and how far you still have to go.

2. Polish the things you're already good at:

We feel confident in the things we know we are good at. Everyone has some kind of strengths, talents, and skills. You just have to recognize what's yours and work towards it to polish it. Some people are naturally good at everything they do. But that doesn't make you any less unique. You have to try to build on those things that you are good at, and they will help you built confidence in your abilities.

3. Set goals for yourself daily:

Whether it's cooking for yourself, reading a book, studying for a test, planning to meet a friend, or doing anything job-related, make a to-do list for yourself daily. Plan the steps that you have to take to achieve them. They don't necessarily have to be big goals; you should always aim for small achievements. At the end of the day, tick off all the things you did. This will help you gain confidence in your ability to get things done and give you a sense of self-appreciation and self-worth.

4. Talk yourself up:

That tiny voice inside of our heads is the key player in the game of our lives. You'll always be running low on confidence if that voice constantly has negative commentary in your mind telling you that you're not good enough. You should sit somewhere calm and quiet and talk to yourself out of all the negative things. Treat yourself like you would treat a loved one when they tend to feel down. Convince yourself that you can achieve anything, and there's nothing that can stop you. Fill your mind with positive thoughts and act on them.

5. Get a hobby:

Find yourself something that really interests you. It can either be photography, baking, writing, reading, anything at all. When you have found yourself something you are passionate about, commit yourself to it and give it a go. Chances are, you will get motivated and build skills more quickly; this will help you gain self-confidence as you would gradually get better at it and feel accomplished. The praises you will get for it will also boost your confidence.

6. Face your fears:

The best way to gain confidence is to face your fears head-on. There's no time to apply for a promotion or ask someone out on a date until you feel confident enough. Practice facing your fears even if it means that you will embarrass yourself or mess up. Remind yourself that it's just an experiment. You might learn that making mistakes or being anxious isn't half as bad as you would have thought. It will help you gain confidence each time you move forward, and it will prevent you from taking any risks that will result in negative consequences.

7. Surround yourself with positive people:

Observe your friends and the people around you. Do they lift you and accept who you are or bring you down and point out your flaws? A man is known by the company he keeps. Your friends should always positively influence your thoughts and attitude and make you feel better about yourself.

8. **Learn To Strike A Balance:**

Self-confidence is not a static measure. Some days, we might feel more confident than others. We might often feel a lack of confidence due to criticism, failures, lack of knowledge, or low self-esteem. While another time we might feel over-confident. We might come off as arrogant and self-centred to other people, and it can eventually lead to our failure. We should keep a suitable amount of confidence within ourselves.

Conclusion:

Confidence is primarily the result of how we have been taught and brought up. We usually learn from others how to behave and what to think of ourselves. Confidence is also a result of our experiences and how we learn to react in different situations. Everyone struggles with confidence issues at one time or another, but these quick fixes should enough to boost your confidence. Start with the easier targets, and then work yourself up. I believe in you. Always!

Chapter 21:
Start Working On Your Dreams Today

When did you get up today? What was your day like? What did you achieve today? Did any of that matter?

Maybe it didn't because you don't have any dreams to work towards, or maybe that you've forgotten what they are altogether.

To have a dream is to have a direction in life. To have a dream means you have something bigger than yourself that you want to achieve.

Everyone gets at least one chance in their life to actually go and pursue that dream, but few recognize that until it is too late. It is too late to regret when you are on your deathbed wondering what could have been. That is when it is too late to work on your dreams. When you have no more time left.

The Moment to start working On your dreams is right here right now.

We repeat our failures every day but never learn. We get depressed every day but never communicate. We get bullied every day, but never fight back. Why?

Is it because we can't do it? No, Definitely Not! We can do it whenever we want. We can do it today. We can do it the next minute. We just lack Ambition!

Every day someone achieves something big. Some more than often, others maybe not their whole life. But the outcome is **not** determined by **fate**, but with **Effort**.

All the billionaires you see today started out with a few dollars just like you and me. They just had the guts to pursue their dream no matter what the cost is. They all had a vision of something bigger. They went full throttle even when everyone around them expected them to fail. Even when they met with struggles that hit them harder than the last, they were still focused on the dream. Never did they once lesson the effort.

No two persons are born the same. Not the same face, color, intelligence, or fate. But what's common for every human being is the built-in trait to strive for a goal once they are determined enough. Doesn't matter if it's food for the next meal or success for the times to come.

The struggle is real, it always was, it always will be. The world wouldn't be what it is today if it weren't for the struggle man has gone through over the centuries. The struggle is the most real definition of life in this world. But that doesn't mean it's a bad one.

Our parents struggled to make us a better person. They put in their best effort to watch us succeed in our dreams. Their parents did the same for them and their parents before them.

This is what makes life a cycle of inherited struggle and hardships. Nobody asks to struggle through a hard life, but we can all turn the hard life into a meaningful one. The life that we all should expect to eventually achieve only if we keep the cycle running and if we keep putting in the effort.

How then do we actually work towards our dreams? By focusing on the things that matter each and every day, again and again, until that mountain has been conquered. Don't forget to enjoy the journey, because it could well be the best part of the trip up top.

You never know what the next moment has in it for you. You can never predict the future, but you can always hope for a better one. You only get the right to hope if you did what was meant to be done today. It's your lawful right to reap the fruit if you took care of sowing the seeds faithfully and diligently all through the year.

The motivation behind this continuous grind of time in search of that Dream lies in your past. You cannot achieve those dreams until you start treasuring the lessons of your past and become a person who is always willing to go beyond.

You can't simply depend on hope to get something done. You have to reach the point where start obsessing over that goal, that thing, that DREAM. When you start obsessing, you start working, you start seeing the possibilities and you just keep going. If you don't get up then you WILL miss the moment. The moment that could have made all the difference in the world. If you don't act upon that impulse, you might never get that inspiration ever again. And that will be the moment you will always regret for the rest of your life.

Remember that your whole life is built on millions of tiny decisions. A decision to just act on one of those moments can transform your life completely. These moments often test you too. But only for an inch more before you find eternal glory. So don't wait for someone else to do it for you. Get up, buckle up, and start doing. Because only you Can!

Chapter 22:

7 Ways On How To Attract Success In Life

Successful people fail more times than unsuccessful people try. A new thought author and metaphysical writer Florence Scovel Shinn in her timeless 1940 novel, 'the secret door to success,' suggests that "Success is not a secret, it is a system." Throughout the centuries, the leaders have alluded to the possibility that success can be attracted into one's life simply by thinking and doing. It is rather a planned journey as we give validity to the premise of creating a plan or setting a goal for ourselves. Goals are set to be achieved, and achievements pave the way for success. Here are 7 Ways To Attract Success In Your Life:

1. **Define What Success Means To You**

Success is subjective to the person who seeks to obtain it, and the ideas may be different for each other. For some of us, success means wealth. For some, it means health and happiness. While for some, it is the mere effort of getting out of bed every day. But the thing that is most highlighted is that we can never get success without struggling. Every one of us wants success, but we do not know how to bring about that life-changing phenomenon that will take us to the zenith of our potential.

2. **Begin with Gratitude:**

From flying to the sky to crashing to the ground, be always thankful to wherever life takes you. Always start by being grateful for what you already have. Whether it's good or bad, we cannot climb the stairs of success without having experiences. If we make mistakes, we should make sure not to give up, rather learn from those mistakes. We must strive to embrace our flaws and imperfections. If we tend to fall seven times, we must have the energy to get up eight times. Whatever life throws us at, no matter the obstacles and challenges, we should always be in a state of gratitude and always be thankful for our learning.

3. Stop making excuses:

Your decisions lead to your destiny. If you are thinking about delaying your work or 'chilling' first, then someone else will take that opportunity for himself. You either grab on the opportunities from both hands, or you sit on the sidelines and watch someone else steal your spotlight. There's no concept of resting and being lazy when you have to work towards your goals and achieve your dreams. One of the major mistakes of unsuccessful people is that they make endless excuses. They would avoid their tasks in any way instead of working on them and actually doing them. You will attract success only if you put your mind towards something and work hard towards it.

4. Realize your potential:

The fine line between incredibly hardworking people and yet fail to achieve success, and the ones who are at the peak of their respective field is simple – potential. We never realize our true potential until we are put in a situation where there's no way out but to express our abilities. We might think that people have more excellent skills than us or have more knowledge than us. But the truth is, we have more potential inside of us. This might be tougher to implement as we don't know how well we can handle things while stressing out or how much hidden talents and skills we possess. Our potential is merely what might make us successful or a failure. It all depends on how much we are willing to try and push ourselves forward.

5. **Celebrate the success of others:**

What you wish upon others finds its way and comes back to you again. While seeing people being successful in their professional and personal lives and making a fortune in their careers and businesses can be tough on our lives, always remember that they too faced struggles and challenges before reaching here. There's no need to be envious as life has an abundance of everything to offer to everyone. Whatever is it in your destiny will always find its way to you. You can't snatch what others have achieved, and similarly, others can't seize whatever that you have or may achieve. Congratulate people around you and be excited for them. Send out positive vibes to everyone so you may receive the same.

6. **Behave as if you are successful:**

Have you heard of the term "fake it till you make it?" Well, it applies to this scenario too. You can fake your success and act like a successful person until you really become one. First, surround yourself with lucrative people. See what habits they have developed over time, how they dress up, how they behave, and, most importantly, how much work they do daily to achieve their goals. Get inspired from them and adopt their healthy habits. Be successful in your own eyes first so that eventually you can be successful in other's eyes as well.

7. **Provide value for others:**

While money and fame are the most common success goals, we should first try to focus on creating value in the world. A lot of successful people wanted to change things in the world first and help people out. Mark Zuckerberg built a tool for Harvard students initially and now has over 1.4 billion users. The first thing on our mind after waking up shouldn't be money or success, and it would be to create value for the world and the people around us.

Conclusion:

It would be best if you strived to explore the unique, endless possibilities within you. Then, when you start working on yourself, you're adding to your mind's youth, vitality, and beauty.

Chapter 23:
<u>10 Habits of Drake</u>

Aubrey Drake Graham, famously known as Drake, was born on 26th October 1986 in Toronto, Canada. Drake was born a musician – a trait from his family roots.

Here are ten habits of Drake:

1. <u>He Identifies Himself With His African Heritage.</u>

Although Drake was born outside Africa, he is proud of the African culture where his father hails from. In an interview, he once said that he considers himself more of a Black man than White.

He is not shy of his African descent. When sharing about his childhood, he recalls that he was raised by his mother in a Jewish setting and he felt out of place in a high school of dominant white people.

2. <u>He Loves Acting.</u>

Drake rose to fame in a teen drama series *Degrassi: The Next Generation* where he played the role of Jimmy Brooks. So great was his passion for acting that he dropped out of school to pursue acting as a career.

He starred in *Degrassi* from 2001 to 2009. This was something Drake as a teen had not envisaged in his life. He landed the acting role after his classmate's father had asked his son to have anyone who made him laugh at school audition for him.

3. <u>He Is Hardworking.</u>

The young Graham managed to build a name for himself just a year after appearing in *Degrassi*. In 2002, he bagged a young artist award. This was the beginning of his star shining brighter.

He has worked hard in his music career and won a Grammy award for the best rap album, *Take care* in 2013. His hard work has put him in a position to mingle with giants in the music industry both in America and Canada.

4. <u>He Has Thick Skin.</u>

Drake has developed a thick skin against scandals in his music career. He once had a bitter rivalry with Chris Brown as they were competing for Rihanna's love. This erupted into violence and both were sued for damages by those who were hurt in the incident.

Nothing has derailed his journey in music. He was once sued by his former girlfriend over her input in co-writing *Marvin's Room*. She was seeking credit for it but Drake managed to settle the matter out of court.

5. <u>He Is Aggressive.</u>

Drake does not take insults lying down. He responds with fire for fire. He has found himself in feuds with Tyga and Meek Mill. In 2015, Meek alleged that Drake was using a ghostwriter for a song they were collaborating.

Drake recorded and released two diss tracks aimed at Meek Mill within a single week. In the following year, he was also in another war of words with Joe Budden.

6. <u>He Has A Strong Determination.</u>

Drake is a strong-willed person and nothing obscures his way to success. They may only delay him but not prevent him from attaining his goals. This led him to release his famous song *Started from the bottom* in 2013 inspired by his struggle for success.

In an interview with MTV News, Drake is quoted saying that he wanted the world to know through that song that he works hard to be successful. It is not a coincidence.

7. <u>He Speaks His Mind.</u>

Only a day after his hit single *Hotline Bling* won a Grammy award for the best rap song in 2017, he did not mince his words to the Grammys for pushing him into the rap category. He publicly declined the award.

It is enviable how he speaks his mind without second thoughts. His outspoken nature has earned him fans and foes alike but still he soldiers on.

8. He Does Not Hold Grudges.

Drake is a man who does not keep a record of wrongs. He was on bad terms with Chris Brown when they were both competing for Rihanna's attention. It is unthinkable that they would later reunite once more.

He reconciled with Chris Brown and they released a hit song, *No Guidance* in 2019. Drake referred to Chris Brown as the most talented human being on the planet. Drake also championed Meek Mill's release from prison and celebrated Mill's release through social media.

9. He Is A Great Songwriter.

Drake knows how to either subtly or directly throw jabs to his target. His songs are always pregnant with a message for his fans.

He has answered his critics on allegations that he uses a ghostwriter for his lyrics through diss tracks. The latest is *Duppy Freestyle* aimed at rapper Pusha T in 2018.

10. He Values Family.

Drake has faced allegations from rapper Pusha T that he is a deadbeat father and he is hiding a child. The following month, Drake confirmed Pusha T's claim. He defended himself that he delayed announcing his son's birth because the paternity test was inconclusive.

However, after it was clear that Adonis was his son, Drake could not hold his joy of being a father. He gushed over the toddler and posted pictures of his nuclear family on Instagram.

In conclusion, these are the ten common habits of Drake both in his public and private life.

Chapter 24:
Happy People Don't Make Excuses

"If you are interested, you'll do what's convenient. If you are committed, you'll do whatever it takes" — John Assaraff.

Read it again. Take it in. This is one of the most effective ideas I recognize in the making and proudly owning your fitness and happiness. Happy humans are dedicated to being satisfied and successful, and much less satisfied humans are normally simplest inquisitive about being satisfied.

The distinction is huge.

What it means is this. When we are truly committed to an outcome — whatever it may be: getting in shape, buying an investment property, qualifying as a vet, owning your own business — we will do whatever it takes to make it happen. There will be obstacles. With any milestone that's big or consequential, a few (or many) obstacles along the way are an inevitable part of that journey. A happy and successful person knows that and moves over or around that obstacle in whatever way they can to keep their eye focused on the outcome they want. They will try and try and try in however many ways they need to to make it happen. They are not just interested in their success, and they are incontrovertibly committed to it. They don't get thrown off at the first sign of struggle.

They are more committed to their goal than they are interested in another 45 minutes in bed or the social acceptance of joining in with a slice of cake.

When we are interested rather than committed, the main thing you will hear coming out of our mouths is excuses. "Oh, I was going to save that money, but something unexpected came up"; "I am getting back on that eating plan as soon as, but it's just been really busy at the moment" that sort of thing.
Excuses. Excuses.

This is the place where my other statement comes in, "Everything before the 'but' is BS." Smart, correct? It summarizes everything for me — everything before the "yet" is what we are keen on, instead of focusing on. On the off chance that we were submitted, there would be no "however." It would be an "and" all things being equal. For instance: "I needed to set aside that cash, something startling came up thus I needed to work three additional movements/offer some stuff to get it going" or "I'm back on that eating plan, it's been truly occupied right now thus I have needed to deny many things to get it going; however, I've done it."

Chapter 25:
10 Habits of Successful Traders

Becoming a successful trader is the dream of every business person. It is the crux of the art of doing business and only a handful of traders attain it. Trade has its ups and downs and a lot is required of you if you are to make it.

Here are ten habits of successful traders:

1. **They Are Well Connected**

Connections could be just what you are lacking for you to have that boom you have yearning. Doing business in urban areas is not a walk in the park. Successful traders seek partnerships with celebrities who help them market their products or services.

When you have a good relationship with influential people, they will channel customer traffic your way. Businesses with public figures as their brand ambassadors are more likely to do well in a highly competitive industry.

2. **They Are Good Managers**

Successful traders believe in themselves managing their trade. It is very difficult to find an unsupervised trustworthy employee who will steer a business to success. This has made successful traders learn to manage their business even if they were armatures at the beginning.

Over time, they manage to perfect their management skills and require external help less often. Management requires practice and successful traders do not give up learning it. Some even enroll in colleges to learn management skills that they will implement in their businesses.

3. <u>They Are Risk-Takers</u>

The art of doing trade sometimes requires extreme decisions involving risks. The return on investment of risky ventures is high, although few traders are ready to wade into such territories. This makes only a handful of traders successful.

Taking calculated risks is the habit of successful traders. They have a backup mechanism to cushion their businesses in the event of an unanticipated loss. The underlying principle in investment is that the higher the risk the higher the returns.

4. <u>They are Knowledgeable About Their Market</u>

Knowledge is power and successful traders use this tool in their businesses. You need accurate and precise information about the market if you want to meet its needs. Successful traders do not sit back to wait for information but instead hunt for it themselves.

With the right data, they implement the right strategies. Unlike merchants who are in business aimlessly, successful traders have relevant information about the market they operate in at their fingertips.

5. <u>They Take Customer Feedback Seriously</u>

Feedback is an important aspect of communication. Serious traders end up successful because they incorporate this in their businesses. They always seek client responses on how they enjoyed their goods or services. Routine asking for feedback is not in vain. It is aimed at improving their services or products for consumer consumption. When clients observe that their feedback was taken seriously, they will be motivated to use their products once more. Feedback is very powerful in sealing the success of any trade.

6. <u>They Conform To The Emerging Trends</u>

The needs of the market are ever-evolving and those in business should learn to evolve with them. This is a common habit of successful traders. They will go the extra mile to provide a new service to meet market demand.

The success of traders in competitive sectors of the economy is pegged on their adapting to new styles. They will be the first to stock clothes in fashion or the latest mobile devices. It is such stock that will move fast and they will realize higher revenues.

7. <u>They Are Patient</u>

Sometimes business could be at a low season. This does not qualify the traders to quit the business. Like everything else, business too has its off-peak days. Great patience is needed to survive this season – a trait successful traders have no shortage of.

Patience is required to grow a business steadily through the stages of growth until it breaks even and starts earning profit. Thereafter, the same business will pass the ceiling and register huge profit margins.

8. <u>They Rarely Give Credit</u>

As much as traders may want to give credit to maintain customer loyalty, the success of a business may not be realized if they overdo it. There are several factors that successful business people consider before allowing credit and being reckless about it is not one of them.

Customer loyalty is not guaranteed because you allow credit. It may make you be bankrupt and close shop. Successful traders give discounts when their clients make purchases instead of giving credit recklessly.

9. <u>They Maintain An Excellent Relationship With Their Suppliers</u>

The relationship between traders and their suppliers is as equally important as that between them and their customers. Successful traders build bridges with their suppliers over time even up to the point of getting goods on credit to sell and pay later.

Such strong relationships with suppliers ensure these traders never run out of stock. Customers will always find goods from their stores and business will run smoothly. This makes a great difference in trade to crown them successful.

10. <u>They Are Law-Abiding</u>

Trade is legitimate in all jurisdictions worldwide except that the items of trade are illegal in that country. This informs the success of a business. It should conform to existing laws and be subject to inspection by authorities.

Successful traders are law-abiding. They pay taxes and seek a license to operate. This insulates their businesses from legal action against them. Their acceptance of regulation will help them remain open when their peers are evading crackdowns on illicit trade. They attract more customers because of their consistency in operation.

In conclusion, successful traders are tied to the hip by these ten habits. They have propelled them to their success. To be successful like they are, implement them and watch your star in trade rise.

Chapter 26:
<u>The Appetite of Success</u>

What is that you want? What are you hungry for? What eats you up on the inside or sets you on fire? Because that is the measure of your success. Not what other people say, not what career they think you should do, nor how much money they think you should make.

Success is satiating the hunger inside of you.

But the appetite of success cannot be fed once. You don't eat one meal and find yourself full for the rest of your life. That would be crazy. You'd find yourself starved and weak. Delirious. I want to tell you that if you are at a loss, if the world seems to be spinning beyond your control then you are probably starving the appetite of success. Meaning is found in purpose, and purpose is fulfilled through action. SO WHY ARE YOU NOT DOING ANYTHING. If you are feeling empty you are the only one who can choose to fill up again. Find the thing that gets you going and start grinding.

Work has become something negative. We seem to think that work is a burden that we have to bear. But that's not what work was supposed to be, work used to be about finding a craft, a skill that you can hone sharper than the blacksmith's blades next door. It was about turning something interesting into something practical, then turning something practical into something sellable. Nothing has changed! Entrepreneurs still do that, people who enjoy their jobs still do that, YOU can still do that!

But you have to make the choice to chase the thing that challenges you, that calls the craftsman inside of you out. Everyone has the potential to be a master at something, but I feel like a lot of people fail to find their pursuit of mastery. In a noisy world it's hard to hear the call, but if you want to achieve success you have to know what success means to you.

You won't satisfy a craving by having anything else other than what you are craving. Then moment you identify what you are hungry for is the moment you can pursue success, understanding your appetite is the first step to mastery.

So, what are you waiting for!?

Search. Experiment. Pick up new hobbies. I don't care what it takes I care about WHERE IT TAKES YOU. You need to wake up excited and go to sleep satisfied.

Annie Dillard once said that,

"How we spend our days is, of course, how we spend our lives."

If you are just waiting around for something to magically happen, it never will. **Success meets on Mondays and it's time you started showing up**. You should be more concerned with the everyday than the one day. Because one day is just the compound of every day. The only way to change what one day looks like, is to change what today looks like. So, GET GOING!

Chapter 27:
Planning Ahead

The topic that are going to discuss today is probably one that is probably not going to apply to everybody, especially for those who have already settled down with a house, wife, kids, a stable career, and so on. But i still believe that we can all still learn something from it. And that is to think about planning ahead. Or rather, thinking long term.

You see, for the majority of us, we are trained to see maybe 1 to 2 years ahead in our lives. Being trained to do so in school, we tend to look towards our next grade, one year at a time. And this system has ingrained in us that we find it hard to see what might and could happen 2 or 3 years down the road.

Whilst there is nothing wrong with living life one year at a time, we tend to fall into a short term view of what we can achieve. We tell ourselves we must learn a new instrument within 1 year and be great at it, or we must get this job in one year and become the head of department, or we must find our partner and get married within a short amount of time. However, life does not really work that way, and things actually do take much longer, and we do actually need more time to grow these small little shoots into big trees.

We fail to see that we might have to give ourselves a longer runway time of maybe 3-5 or even 10 years before we can become masters in a new instrument, job, relationship, or even friendships. Rome isn't built in a day and we shouldn't expect to see results if we only allow ourselves 1 year to accomplish those tasks. Giving ourselves only 1 year to achieve the things we want can put unnecessary pressure on ourselves to expect results fast, when in reality no matter how much you think u think rushing can help you achieve results faster, you might end up burning yourself out instead.

For those short term planners, even myself. I have felt that at many stages in my life, i struggle to see the big picture. I struggle to see how much i can achieve in lets say 5 years if i only allowed myself that amount of time to become a master in whatever challenge i decide to take on. Even the greatest athletes take a longer term view to their career. They believe that if they practice hard each day, they might not expect to see results in the first year, but as their efforts compound, by the 5th year they would have already done so much practice that it is statistically impossible not to be good at it.

And when many of us fall into the trap of simply planning short term, our body reacts by trying to rush the process as well. We expect everything to be fast fast fast, and results to be now now now. And we set unrealistic goals that we cannot achieve and we beat ourselves up for it come December 31st.

Instead i believe many of us should plan ahead by giving ourselves a minimum of 2.5 years in whatever task we set to achieve, be it an income goal, a fitness goal, or a relationship goal. 2.5 years is definitely much more manageable and it gives us enough room to breathe so that we don't stress ourselves out unnecessarily. If you feel like being kinder to yourself, you might even give yourselves up to 5 years.

And again the key to achieving success with proper long term planning is Consistency. If you haven't watched my video on consistency do check it out as i believe it is one of the most important videos that I have ever created.

I believe that with a run time of 5 years and consistency in putting the hours every single day, whether it is an hour or 10 hours, that by the end of it, there is no goal that you cannot achieve. And we should play an even longer game of 10 years or so. Because many of the changes we want to make in life should be permanent and sustainable. Not a one off thing.

So I challenge each and everyone of you today to not only plan ahead, but to think ahead of the longevity of the path that you have set for yourself. There is no point rushing through life and missing all the incredible sights along the way. I am sure you will be a much happier person for it.

Chapter 28:
How to Learn Faster

Remember the saying, "You are never too old to learn something new"? Believe me, it's not true in any way you understood it.

The most reliable time to learn something new was the time when you were growing up. That was the time when your brain was in its most hyperactive state and could absorb anything you had thrown at it.

You can still learn, but you would have to change your approach to learning.

You won't learn everything, because you don't like everything going on around you. You naturally have an ego to please. So what can you do to boost your learning? Let's simplify the process. When you decide to learn something, take a moment and ask yourself this; "Will this thing make my life better? Will this fulfill my dreams? Will I benefit from it?".

If you can answer all these questions in a positive, you will pounce on the thing and you won't find anyone more motivated than you.

Learning is your brain's capability to process things constructively. If you pick up a career, you won't find it hard to flourish if you are genuinely interested in that particular skill.

Whether it be sports, singing, entrepreneurship, cooking, writing, or anything you want to pursue. Just ask yourself, can you use it to increase your creativity, your passion, your satisfaction. If you can, you will start learning it as if you knew it all along.

Your next step to learning faster would be to improve and excel at what you already have. How can you do that? It's simple yet again!

Ask yourself another question, that; "Why must I do this? Why do I need this?" if you get to answer that, you will find the fastest and effective way to the top yourself without any coaching. Why will this happen on its own? Because now you have found a purpose for your craft and the destination is clear as the bright sun in the sky.

The last but the most important thing to have a head start on your journey of learning is the simplest of them all, but the hardest to opt for. The most important step is to start working towards things.

The flow of learning is from Head to Heart to Hands. You have thought of the things you want to do in your brain. Then you asked your heart if it satisfied you. Now it's time to put your hands to work.

You never learn until you get the chance to experience the world yourself. When you go through a certain event, your brain starts to process the outcomes that could have been, and your heart tells you to give it one more try. Here is the deciding moment. If you listen to your heart right away, you will get on a path of learning that you have never seen before.

What remains now is your will to do what you have decided. And when you get going, you will find the most useful resources immediately. Use your instincts and capitalize your time. Capture every chance with sheer will and belief as if this is your final moment for your dreams to come true.

It doesn't matter if you are not the ace in the pack, it doesn't matter if you are not in your peak physical shape, it doesn't matter if you don't have the money yet. You will someday get all those things only if you had the right skills and the right moment.

For all you know, this moment right now is the most worth it moment. So don't go fishing in other tanks when you have your own aquarium. That aquarium is your body, mind, and soul. All you need is to dive deep with sheer determination and the stars are your limit.

Chapter 29:
6 Habits To Impress Your Boss and Thrive

It is still unclear to a majority of people what their bosses and employers want from them. Some expressly make it crystal to their employees their expectations of them while others are reserved. What is clear though, is that bosses worldwide have a common goal – to make a profit. It is the major reason why they hired people in their companies to work for them. Many employees wrongly believe that unless their superiors make a complaint against them, then their work is satisfactory. This notion is a fallacy. Satisfactorily is not the threshold of competency but uniqueness and creativity.

Here are six common habits to impress your boss and thrive:

1. Be Unique And Creative

The question employees fail to answer honestly is what they bring to the table. What is it that makes you stand out in the company you work for? It is not your education level because there are many qualified learned people with your skills. Neither is it the duration you work in the company because you receive remuneration for it.

You should be creative in your work and add value to the company. Your devotion to your work will impress your boss because it is uncommon.

Ideally, you ought to be irreplaceable in your workplace for you to gain favor and earn a promotion.

2. Ensure Proper Communication

Communication is the master key to unlocking conflicts and misunderstandings at the workplace. It is important to ensure proper communication with your boss in your working relationship. You will be able to explain yourself and raise any pertinent issue that affects your work if you have good communication with them.

When you communicate effectively, your superiors will understand you better than if you have poor communication skills or none at all. It may come out as rudeness or ignorance when you communicate ineffectively with your boss. To thrive and gain favor with him/her, build on your communication.

3. Never Outshine Your Master

In his famous book, *48 laws of power,* Robert Greene writes this as his first law. It is prudent never to outshine your master and instead let him appear smarter than you are even if it may not be the case. This speaks life to the respect of hierarchy between your boss and yourself. Never make him appear dumb or lame duck by attracting glory to yourself.

Honor your boss both in your speech and in your actions. This will make you find favor in their eyes and you will thrive in your workplace. It does not imply that you should not give any smart suggestions to your bosses but you should do it in a manner that does not usurp their authority.

4. <u>Have Integrity</u>

Integrity is the quality of honesty and transparency that one may have. You are misplaced and out of order if your boss cannot trust you to do a task without supervision. Worse is that you are in a bad light if you fall short of honesty and cannot be trusted with the management of resources.

Leaders and bosses are universally interested in people of integrity who will fairly work for them. They want people they will trust to oversee the rest and take their organizations to the next level. The lack of integrity is the biggest turn-off for bosses no matter how qualified employees could be. Uphold integrity to impress your boss and you shall thrive.

5. <u>Share Their Vision For The Company</u>

The hiring of managers is tedious and sometimes the competent candidates could not be having the passion of the business at heart. Their remunerations could be their greatest motivation. Routine checks and job evaluations could reveal such hidden traits in employees.

Nevertheless, you need to share the vision of the company with your employer for them to trust you with their resources. People who share the company vision impress hiring managers and owners because their salary is not the sole motivation to work.

6. <u>Be Punctual</u>

It is prudent to be punctual in your job. Punctuality is the act of being on time, never late for anything. You should report to work on time, complete assigned tasks on time, and even submit reports required from you on time.

Being punctual is a sign of dedication to your job. This act alone will make your boss have a soft spot for you.

In conclusion, when you develop these six habits, you will impress your boss and thrive at your workplace.

Chapter 30:
The Struggle With Time

Today we're going to talk about a topic that isn't commonly looked at in depth. But it is one that we might hopefully find a new appreciation for. And that is TIME.

Time is a funny thing, we are never really aware of it and how much of a limited resource it really is until we get a rude awakening. Most commonly when our mortality is tested. Whether it be a health scare, an accident, a death of a loved one, a death of a pet, we always think we have more time before that. That we will always have time to say i love you, to put off the things we always told ourselves we needed to do, to start making that change, to spend time with the people that mean the most to us.

As we go about our days, weeks and months, being bothered and distracted by petty work, by our bosses, colleagues, trying to climb the corporate ladder, we forget to stop and check in on our fiends and family... We forget that their time may be running out, and that we may not have as much time with them as we think we do, until it is too late, and then we regret not prioritising them first. All the money that we made could not ever buy back the time we have lost with them. And that is something we have to live with if we ever let that happen.

The other funny thing about time is that if we don't set it aside for specific tasks, if we don't schedule anything, we will end up wasting it on something mindless. Whether it be browsing social media endlessly, or bingeing on television, we will never run out of things to fill that time with. Can you imagine that even though time is so precious, we willingly sacrifice and trade it in for self isolation in front of our TVs and computers for hours on end. Sometimes even for days? Or even on mobile games. Some being so addictive that it consumes most of our waking hours if we are not careful.

Our devices have become dangerous time wasters. It is a tool Shea its literally sapping the living energy out of us. Which is why some responsible companies have started implementing new features that help us keep track of our screen time. To keep us in check, and to not let our children get sucked into this black hole that we might struggle to climb out of.

I believe the biggest struggle with time that we all have is how to spend it in such a way that we can be happy without feeling guilty. Guilty of not spending it wisely. And I believe the best way to start is to start defining the things that you need to do, and the things that you want to do. And then striking a balance. To set equal amounts of time into each activity so that it doesn't overwhelm or underwhelm you. Spend one hour on each activity each day that you feel will have an impact on your life in a meaningful way, and you can spend your time on television or games without remorse.

So I challenge each of you to make the most of your time. SPending time with loved ones always come first, followed by your goals and dreams, and then leisure activities. Never the other way around. That way you can be at the end of your life knowing that you had not wasted the most precious commodity that we are only given a finite amount of. Money can't buy back your youth, your health, or time with loved ones, so don't waste it.

I believe in each and everyone of you, take care, and as always ill see you in the next one.

Chapter 31:
The Power of Growing 1% Each Day

We all chase growth, we all chase success, but many of us want to be the best overnight, we want to get better 1000% over a month. We expect to lose 50 pounds by the end of the month, so we push ourselves so hard, so fast, so intensely, that we often burn out before the month has even ended.

We apply this same speed to our relationships, our careers, other aspects of our health, and we soon wonder why we cannot sustain this momentum for long.

The reason is that changes must be made gradually. Sure we can go cold turkey by cutting carbs out completely from our diet, but how many of you will agree that by the 4th day, many of us will start bingeing on that big plate of pasta because we just miss it so much.

If instead, we had cut our portions of pasta quota for the week by say 30%, how many of you would agree that it would have been a much better route to take instead of the former?

Today I want to challenge you to totally reframe how you approach change. After you have identified the areas in your life you know you need to work on, I want you to start working on one aspect at a time.

Instead of aiming for a 100% growth and transformation by the end of next week, I want you to tell yourself that you will be a 1% better version of yourself each and every day.

This mindset immediately alleviates any pressure we have on ourselves for drastic changes. Changes that are unsustainable even in the short run. By making incremental changes, we give ourselves the space to grow, to learn, to get better, and to be better.

Take your favourite sport for example. For me it's tennis. I don't expect to become like Federer overnight no matter how hard I believe I can. Instead, i break down each aspect of federer's game and work on fine adjustments to my own game 1% at a time. These 1% gains will compound over time. As with everything else that you do.

If career is an area of focus for you, instead of expecting to become employee of the month by the next month, work instead on becoming a 1% better employee each day. By the end of 100 days, you would've already become more than 100% than you were at the start of your job, and by the end of the year, you would already be so amazing at it that you would've believe how you got there in the first place.

Life is a marathon, not a sprint. If we sprint through life, we will miss all the amazing sights along the way. We will miss the fine details that make the journey worth taking. Similarly, our personal development and growth is also a marathon, not a sprint. We should all keep that in perspective when we approach any new project or endeavour. Only then can we truly make a lasting difference in the areas of our lives that matters to us most.

Chapter 32:
How To Take Note of Your Flaws

We all have flaws. As much as we can try to pretend we are perfect, we will find out soon enough from life that we all have parts of us that fall short in one way or another.

This doesn't mean that we are inferior, rather that we have room for improvement. By reframing our flaws as areas of growth, we can change the way we see our weaknesses.

But before we can grow, we first need to identify exactly what areas in our lives that we actually need to work on. It is easy for many of us to go through our days without thinking too much about the important aspects that we are failing to address. And when the time comes for us to perform, we wonder why we always come up short.

We then berate ourselves and assume that we are no good or that we are worse than others. All because we were not acute and aware enough to work on our flaws consistently over a period of time.

If health is an issue for us, either because we feel we are not getting to our ideal weight or sugar level, or whatever it may be, we need to note the habits that are bringing us down and work to replace them with healthier ones that bring us good instead.

We do this, again, by the power of journaling. Only through journaling can we realize exactly how much we are eating, how many calories we are actually consuming each meal, and how can we replace or reduce our intake to reach our goals.

It is easy for us to assume each meal is independent of the other. But everything we consume adds up. A can of coke might not seem much in one sitting, but 3 cans over the course of the day can quickly add up.

By journaling each activity we are doing, writing down the aspects that we excelled at and ones where we fall short at, we can identify the exact mistakes that we are making in order to improve on them gradually each day.

As the saying goes, practice makes perfect. We don't expect to ace the test on the first try, so why should we expect our flaws to be corrected on the second if we do nothing to improve it?

Once we become painfully aware of every single action we are taking, we can then work backwards and deconstruct each activity To find the areas we can work on.

Trust me, Rome isn't built in a day, so taking note and taking action on your flaws is the only way you will see any long-term progress in anything that you do in life. Take care, I believe in you, and I'll see you in the next one.

Chapter 33:
<u>10 Habits of David Beckham</u>

David Robert Joseph Beckham, famously known as only David Beckham, was born on 2nd May 1975 in Leytonstone, East London, England to Ted and Sandra Beckham. He is the only son in his family between two sisters. His family members were staunch fans of Manchester United. He showed interest in football while he was still a child and started charting his path as a professional soccer player.

Here are ten habits of David Beckham:

1. <u>He is a great leader.</u>

David is a great leader both in the pitch and outside. He was the England national team captain from 2000 to 2006. During his tenure, he led England to the World Cup in 2002 and 2006. He singlehandedly scored against Greece to qualify England for the World Cup in 2002.

The Briton soccer star addressed the Discovery Leadership Summit in Johannesburg in 2016. He was among key speakers in the summit themed on leadership in business, government, and civil society.

2. <u>He is philanthropic.</u>

Beckham is involved in many charity drives. He has been the goodwill ambassador of the United Nations Children's Fund (UNICEF) since 2005. He champions the good welfare of children globally campaigning on issues affecting children like malnutrition, emergencies, child violence, and abuse.

He founded 7: The David Beckham UNICEF Fund that has changed the lives of vulnerable children globally. He has a personal commitment to secure the future of children and woo world leaders to his cause.

3. <u>He knows when and where to stop.</u>

The former football legend knows his limits and how to make things work for him. He voluntarily retired from playing professional football in May 2013 after 21 years in the game. David understood when to take a break in his career and venture into other activities.

He resisted the temptation of adding an extra year to his contract at Paris Saint-Germain. He was thankful to the French club for allowing him to play for them until the time that he was leaving.

4. <u>He values family.</u>

Beckham adores family ties above everything else. In his retirement speech, he appreciated his family for their sacrifice and support in realizing his dreams. This shows the connection between David and his family.

David said that he owes everything to his wife and children for inspiring him to play for a very long time. Family is most definitely at the heart of the former football icon.

5. <u>He is a businessman.</u>

Apart from soccer, Beckham has ventured into other businesses. He co-owns Beckham brand holdings and Kent & Curwen. These businesses have made him worth over $500 million. He ranks among the wealthiest sportsmen in England.

His retirement from paid soccer has made him engage fully in his businesses. He launched an underwear line for H&M in 2012 and modeled wearing them. They are sold in stores in 40 countries worldwide.

6. <u>He is patriotic.</u>

David Beckham has traveled vastly across the world but he has always maintained his fidelity to his country. He started playing football in England's Manchester United youth league and proceeded to its training division before joining the main club as a full-time starter. It was later in his career that he played for Real Madrid, a Spanish team.

He received a royal award – order of British empire – from the queen on 27th November 2003 for his professional services to the nation. The Queen and Beckham exchanged a few words and she told him it was an honor for her to award the British star.

7. <u>He is an investor.</u>

Besides doing business, David Beckham is an investor. He has a 10% stake in Lunaz, a car restoration and electrification firm based in Britain. He is also a co-owner of a virtual sports academy, Guild Esports.

The former English player is an investor in the Major League Soccer (MLS) and invested a further $ 15.3 million to strengthen the team ahead of the second season. He has taken a keen interest in the sport passively after his retirement.

8. <u>He is a good ambassador.</u>

Beckham has partnered with many firms and endorsed their products. His celebrity status has earned him favor with the world and he has many fans who will use the products he uses without question.

According to Forbes, David's sponsors include Adidas, Coty, H&M, Samsung, and Breitling. He was an ambassador for the Chinese super league in 2013. He is an active and competent ambassador for the brands he represents.

9. <u>He loves acting.</u>

Besides his long sports career, David Beckham is also an actor. He has appeared in *Uncle's Man* directed by Ritchie in 2015. He also played the character of Trigger in the famous 2017 movie – *King Arthur: Legend of the sword*.

By his self-admission, he does not take acting as a career but as a hobby. His fans have enjoyed the movies he has acted in and encouraged him to keep on entertaining them.

10. <u>He enjoys public attention.</u>

Beckham has always been intimate with the attention he has been receiving. His life has always been an open book to the world. Fans once thronged him wanting to take selfies with the football legend when he had gone for lunch with Garry Neville and Ryan Giggs.

He enjoyed the attention he received and took photos with his fans before entering his car and leaving the scene. This is expected of him because he has grown up in the public limelight from his childhood to adulthood.

In conclusion, these ten habits of the former English footballer have majorly defined his lifestyle.

Chapter 34:
How To Live In The Moment

Today we're going to talk about a different topic related to living in the moment. And this one has to do with those going through a health crisis or has a loved one who is going through one.

I hope that by the end of this video, that I will be able to encourage all of you to look at your life differently and look at how you treat your loved one who is going through a health issue with renewed eyes and perspective. Some of these concepts I derived from inspirational figures who have taught me some valuable lessons as well with their strength and resilience.

I know health can be a touchy subject. But i believe that it is something that we all struggle with at some point in our lives. When we are faced with a health scare or crisis, we will suddenly become aware of our own mortality and how fragile our lives really are. And then we start to worry about what might happen and what could happen if this and this occurs, if my health deteoriates, what that will look like, and we start scaring ourselves to no end and we start living our lives in fear that doing simple things become such a challenge for us.

I have had my fair share of health challenges. And I start worrying about the possible degradation of my body, of getting weaker, or getting old, or whatever, and get stuck in this mindset of worry. And we all know that we must not live our lives in fear, because fear is something we cannot really control. And what might happen to us is also not within our control.

What we can control however, when faced with a reality check in a health crisis, is to take stock once again of our life, the choices that we have made, health wise, eating the right foods, getting enough rest, and start fixing those things. Those are the things we can control. Another thing that is fully within our control, is to remember to live our lives in the present. When we realize time is not infinite, we need to remember to treasure each day without fear, and to start doing things now today that we won't regret. To start appreciating each day, savoring every sunset and sunrise, spending time with friends and family, and to never let ourselves get complacent with that. That we don't need multiple health scares in our lives to be reminded to live in the present and to life for the things that matter. You can't bring money with you when you die, but you can bring all your wonderful experiences at the end of your life and tell yourself that it is a life worth living. That is just me reminding u of what it might be like at the end of everyone's life, which is inevitable, this has got nothing to do with your health crisis that you are facing. I just want to be clear on that.

Another very very important thing that we need to be aware of is how we view our loved ones who are going through their own health crisis. If they have been diagnosed with something serious, and that time is of the essence, we need to show support to them by going through life with them to the fullest by spending time with them each and every day in the present moment. Live in the present with them and not worry about what could possibly happen to them. That this very second is magical with them and in this second they are alive and well. Who knows when their health could turn for the worst, and it doesn't really matter. They could live a longer life than you think. But the reality is that we never really know. And we should just cherish the present. I was inspired by this girl who suffered a terminal illness, Claire Wineland. She lived in such bravery and wisdom that she reminded everyone around her including her mom and myself, that in this moment, life is beautiful. That in this moment, life is amazing. And that in this moment, you are amazing.

So i just want to leave it as that. I hope you have been inspired today to live in the moment, in spite of fear, worries, health scares, career problems, and whatever little or big things that are weighing you down today. I hope you never forget how special this very second is.

www.ingramcontent.com/pod-product-compliance
Lightning Source LLC
LaVergne TN
LVHW010348070526
838199LV00065B/5804